Her House Is Built On Prayer

Dr. Rico A. Wagner

REJOICE
Essential Publishing

Dr. Rico A. Wagner/Rejoice Essential Publishing

PO BOX 512

Effingham, SC 29541

www.republishing.org

Author's website: https://ricowagner.com

Unless otherwise indicated, scripture is taken from the King James Version.'

The Holy Bible, English Standard Version (ESV) is adapted from the Revised Standard Version of the Bible, copyright Division of Christian Education of the National Council of the Churches of Christ in the U.S.A. All rights reserved.

Her House Is Built On Prayer/Dr. Rico A. Wagner

ISBN-13: 978-1-956775-95-2

Dedication

I DEDICATE THIS TO MY clan, my family, and my dearest husband, Sammie Wagner Jr., who is the rock of our family, who has taught me the word of God, and who has pulled out the best in me! Thank you for your guidance and for being the prophetic voice in my life.

To our amazing children, Samayah, Stephon, Tyler, Ian, and Ace Wagner, and my daughter-in-law, Shiann, thank you for allowing me just to be me.

Table of Contents

Acknowledgements

A SPECIAL THANKS TO MY beautiful Mother, Nova Irving, who has always provided me with support, guidance, advice, and plenty of laughter. Mom, you taught me early in my life how to be a godly wife and mother and I am extremely grateful.

Foreword

WORDS FROM MY SPIRITUAL Mother, Dr. Donna Houpe

When we become awake, we realized how asleep we have been. To awaken to your real purpose, you must purpose to meet the real creator - God, the Father. When we are awakened, the sun shines brighter, the skies appear clearer, and the ride begins.

Charity begins when you are awakened to the fact that life does not stand still. Therefore, start moving!

It's time for you all to be AWAKENED!

— *Dr. Donna Houpe*

****

I believe prayer is essential in our relationship with God and walk of faith. I remember when I first met my wife, Rico Wagner, she wouldn't go anywhere without praying or reading a scripture. I was amazed at her consistency of including the Lord in her day-to-day life. After 27 years of marriage and co-laboring with her in ministry, one of her greatest strengths is prayer. I remember when she would pray for certain things and the manifestation of what she prayed would show up. I would say to her, "God really hears your prayers." It reminded me of Apostle James saying that the effectual fervent prayer of a righteous man avails much power and is effective (*James 5:16b*).

But one thing I've learned was she would pray from the heart and the will of God as to why her prayers got answered. I believe this book will give you some key points on targeting areas of your life that need to be saturated in prayer, giving you confidence and clarity. Prayer changes your life and creates a close intimacy with God and when answered, it's an outward testimony of having faith in God. I pray that prayer transforms your home (where you live) and your heart (where Jesus lives).

—*Apostle Sammie Wagner*

Introduction

*J*UST SO I'M CLEAR that you know what you're getting into.......
This prayer book is a bit different from others. You are unique and so is this book! We are Re-constructing your mindset and Re-constructing your house into a home built on prayer.

By the time you finish reading and working through this book, something should break or awaken inside of you. The front cover of this book shouldn't be able to close neatly back over on itself. It should be noticeably disfigured from heartfelt use and an impossible option for re-gifting for a Christmas gift. Some pages may be ripped out literally and written on. The edges should have curled corners. Some parts of this book should be bookmarked, so you may have to revisit it.

I invite you to fully engage in every minute of the study. Don't allow any distractions to keep you off course as you build your house with prayer. Let's Go!

CHAPTER 1

Building The Foundation

OUR SPIRITUAL HOUSE HAS to be in order for anyone to see things tangibly in our lives. There must be an inward transformation of the heart from understanding God's will.

The heart is where it all begins, from receiving salvation to developing a relationship with God through prayer to communicating with Him. Let's look at how praying the will of God can birth confidence while praying.

The Apostle John says, *"And this is the confidence we have in approaching God: that if we ask anything according to his will, he hears us. And if we know that he hears us-whatever we ask-we know that we have what we asked of him". — 1 John 5:4-5 NIV.*

The heart is where we believe and speak as we pray to God for guidance, deeper intimacy with Him, and understanding of our purpose since He knows the plans for our lives.

In our time of prayer we need to meditate on God's precepts and allow them to minister to our hearts. Prayer is a two-way conversation from your heart to God's ears. He desires to hear our prayers from a pure heart that is free from offense and unforgiveness. Having offense and unforgiveness can prevent your faith from working and prayers from being answered.

Unforgiveness breeds bitterness and destructive emotions. So be sure to examine your heart according to the holy scriptures to make sure your heart is in the right place before the Lord. Below are some scriptures that will help you obtain results.

Ephesians 4:31-32 says, "Get rid of all bitterness, rage, anger, harsh words, and slander, as well as all types of evil behavior. Instead, be kind to each other, tenderhearted, forgiving one another, just as God through Christ has forgiven you."

Psalm 4:1 ESV says, "Answer me when I call, O God of my righteousness! You have given me relief when I was in distress. Be gracious to me and hear my prayer!"

Psalm 39:12 ESV says "Hear my prayer, O Lord, and give ear to my cry; hold not your peace at my tears! For I am a sojourner with you, a guest, like all my fathers."

Psalm 66:19 ESV says, "But truly God has listened; he has attended to the voice of my prayer."

Psalm 69:13 ESV says, "But as for me, my prayer is to you, O Lord. At an acceptable time, O God, in the abundance of your steadfast love answer me in your saving faithfulness."

Proverbs 15:29 ESV says, "The LORD is far from the wicked, but he hears the prayer of the righteous."

No matter what season we face, the manifestation of what we are believing for shows itself in response to my faith when we speak is what we live and it begins to manifests itself.
— Dr. Rico A. Wagner

1. How can you improve your prayer life?

_____

_____

_____

_____

_____

_____

_____

_____

_____

2. What does it mean if someone prays for you?

_____

_____

_____

_____

_____

_____

_____

_____

_____

_____

For the Christian woman, praying for others really means something. It's more than words and more than a kind thing to say. It does something. God hears and responds when we pray for one another. When we pray for one another, we pray to the same Father on behalf of our brother or sister in Christ.

3. What happens when a woman prays?

_____

_____

_____

_____

_____

_____

_____

_____

_____

_____

_____

When women pray, strongholds are broken, circumstances are changed, healing takes place, and miracles happen. Throughout history, women have stood strong at the forefront of monumental change, and it starts with women warriors kneeling in prayer.

A wise woman builds her house. *Psalm 127:1-2 says, "Unless the LORD builds the house, its builders labor in vain."* This means that if we don't have the Lord's guidance and direction, then our efforts won't yield any results. We need His help to build a good home!

4. Why write the scripture on the walls?

_____

_____

_____

_____

_____

_____

_____

_____

_____

_____

_____

Writing down a scripture on the wall of your new construction is like writing down your own vision for your family and for how you want to be spending your time in that space.

CHAPTER 2

Scriptures For Blessing Your Home

Proverbs 24:3-4 says, "By wisdom, a house is built, and through understanding, it is established; through knowledge, its rooms are filled with rare and beautiful treasures."

Matthew 7:24 says, "Therefore, everyone who hears these words of mine and puts them into practice is like a wise man who built his house on the rock."

Psalm 51:10 says, "Create in me a clean heart, O God, and renew a right spirit within me."

2 Chronicles 7:15-16 says, "Now my eyes will be open and my ears attentive to the prayer that is made in this place. For now, I have chosen and consecrated this house that my name may be there forever. My eyes and my heart will be there all time."

A wise woman doesn't take anything for granted. She is thankful to be loved and seeks to make herself more lovely.

A wise woman doesn't allow herself to be a liability but strives to be an asset to the marriage bond. She looks for ways to make, save, and use money wisely. Her husband knows he is a richer man because she is his wife.

A wise woman seeks to be a part of her husband's life. His interest becomes her interest. She looks for ways to help him in every endeavor in which he is involved. When he needs a helping hand, it is her hand that is there first.

A wise woman knows that his peace of mind (and sometimes, wise understanding) is something she can give or take away from her observations and conversations concerning circumstances or people. She limits her conversation to the positive.

A wise woman sets a joyful mood in the household. She uses laughter, music, and happy times to stir the children into a positive, joyful frame of mind. She knows this light-heartedness helps take stress off her husband. A wise woman surveys her husband's needs. She seeks to fulfill his desires before even he is aware of them. She never leaves him daydreaming outside the home. She supplies his every desire.

A wise woman understands that her husband's need to be honored is not based on his performance but on his position. She learns quickly to defer with enthusiasm to his ideas or plans. She looks for ways to reverence him. She knows this is God's will for her life.

A wise woman is not pitiful, puny, or whiny. She seeks to be confident, capable, and thankful. A wise woman does not dream of what "could have been." She sees clearly that she is not God's gift to men; thus, she is blessed in her present circumstances. She learns to be content.

A wise woman never expects anyone to serve her; therefore, she is never disappointed. She is ready to serve. By her example, her children learn to serve cheerfully and energetically.

A wise woman doesn't interrogate her husband. Her questions are sincere inquiries concerning his will.

A wise woman is always learning. She is open to change. She is ready to hear. She wants to know. She doesn't cloud her mind with the foolish folly of entertainment. She uses her time wisely.

CHAPTER 3

Let's Build! Construction Has Started!

*O*UTSIDE YOUR HOUSE: HEBREWS *3:4 says, "For every house is built by someone, but the builder of all things is God."*

Your Front Door:
Luke 10:5 says, "Peace be to this house."

Your Entry (foyer):
Deuteronomy 28:6 says, "You will be blessed when you go in and blessed when you go out."

Psalm 91:11 says, "For He will command His angels concerning you to guard you in all your ways;"

Proverbs 3:5-6 says, "Trust in the Lord with all your heart and lean not on your own understanding; in all your ways acknowledge Him, and He will make your paths straight."

Psalm 121:8 says, "The Lord will keep you from all evil; he will keep you safe. He will protect you as you come and go, now and forever."

Your Kitchen:

A kitchen is a very important part of any home. It is where most families spend time together as a family unit. We want this space to be a place where everyone feels comfortable and at ease. A kitchen is a place where we prepare meals for ourselves and others.

Acts 2:46 says, "They broke bread together and ate together with glad and sincere hearts."

Hebrews 13:2 says, "Do not forget to entertain strangers, for by doing so, some people have entertained angels without knowing it."

Matthew 6:25 says, "Therefore I tell you, do not worry about your life, what you will eat or drink; nor about your body, what you will wear. Is not life more important than food, and the body more important than clothes?"

Matthew 5:6 says, "Blessed is those who hunger and thirst after righteousness, for they shall be filled."

Matthew 15:34 says, "And he said unto them, how many loaves have ye? And they said, Seven, and a few little fishes."

Your Home Hallways:
Psalms 119:105 says, "Your word is a lamp unto my feet and a light into my path."

Your Living Room:
Joshua 24:15 says, "As for me and my house, we will serve the Lord."

Your Fireplace:

Jeremiah 20:9 says, "His Word is in my heart like a fire shut up in my bones."

Loft:

I imagine the loft will be a space where we will be spending lots of time, playing, reading, and watching. It should be a very cozy spot. We chose these scriptures because they talk about being at home and enjoying the company of others.

My vision for the space is *James 1:19 which says, "Let every person be quick to hear, slow to speak, slow to anger."*

Matthew 6:33 says, "But seek first the kingdom of God and His righteousness, and all these things shall be added unto you."

Colossians 3:12-13 says, "Put on, therefore, as the elect of God, holy and beloved, bowels of mercies, kindness, humbleness of mind, meekness, longsuffering; forbearing one another, and forgiving one another, if any man has a quarrel against any: even as Christ forgave you, so do ye also."

Your Master Bedroom:

The master bedroom is usually reserved for the couple. It is a place where couples spend most of their time together. The bedroom is a sacred space which means that it should be treated as such.

Matthew 19:5 says, "For this cause shall a man leave father and mother and shall cleave to his wife: and the two shall become one flesh."

1 Corinthians 13:4 says, "Love is patient, love is kind."

Ephesians 5:25 says, "Husbands, love your wives, just as Christ loved the church and gave himself up for her."

Psalm 4:8 says, "In peace, I will lie down and sleep, for you alone, Lord, make me dwell in safety."

Song of Solomon 3:4 ESV says, "Scarcely had I passed them when I found him whom my soul loves. I held him, and would not let him go until I had brought him into my mother's house, and into the chamber of her who conceived me.

Your Children's Bedroom:

Writing scriptures for each kid's room is a special way to write down your vision for their life. If they are older, you can also ask them to choose their favorite Bible verse and write it themselves.

Mark 12:30 says, "And you shall love the Lord your God with all your heart and with all your soul and with all your mind."

Psalm 127:3 says, "Children are a gift from the Lord."

Proverbs 22:6 says, "Train up a child in the way he should go, even when he is old, he will not depart from it."

Romans 8:28 says, "And we know that all things work together for good to those who love God, to those who are called according to His purpose."

1 Timothy 4:12 says, "Let no man despise thy youth; but be thou an example of the believers, in word, in conversation, in charity, in spirit, faith, in purity."

Numbers 6:24-26 says, "The Lord bless you and keep you; the Lord make his face to shine upon you and be gracious to you; the Lord lift up his countenance upon you and give you peace."

Proverbs 3:24 says, "When thou liest down, thou shalt not be afraid: yea, thou shalt lie down, and thy sleep shall be sweet."

Psalms 127:3 says, "Lo, children are an heritage of the LORD: and the fruit of the womb is his reward."

Proverbs 3:14 says, "For the merchandise of it is better than the merchandise of silver, and the gain thereof than fine gold."

Deuteronomy 28:6 says, "You will be blessed when you go in and blessed when you go out."

Psalm 4:8 says, "In peace, I will lie down and sleep, for you alone, Lord, make me dwell in safety."

1 John 4:19 says, "We love because He first loved us."

Proverbs 3:24 says, "When you lie down, you will not be afraid; when you lie down, your sleep will be sweet."

Your Closets:

Women: *Proverbs 31 says, "She is more precious than rubies. She is clothed with strength and dignity, and she laughs without fear of the future."*

Men:

Joshua 1:9 says, "Be strong and courageous. Do not be frightened or discouraged, for the Lord, your God is with you wherever you go."

Colossians 3:14 says, "And above all these put-on love, which binds everything together in perfect harmony."

Matthew 6:25 says, "Therefore I tell you, do not worry about your life, what you will eat or drink;

nor about your body, what you will wear. Is not life more important than food, and the body more important than clothes?"

Your Bathroom:

1 Peter 3:3-4 says, "Do not let your adorning be external—the braiding of hair and the putting on of gold jewelry, or the clothing you wear— but let your adorning be the hidden person of the heart with the imperishable beauty of a gentle and quiet spirit, which in God's sight is very precious."

Your Laundry Room:

Psalms 51:7 says, "Purge me with hyssop, and I shall be clean; wash me, and I shall be whiter than snow."

Psalms 51:1-2 says, "Have mercy on me, O God, according to your steadfast love; according to your abundant mercy blot out my transgressions. Wash me thoroughly from my iniquity and cleanse me from my sin!"

Your Home Office:

The home office is a space where we conduct our business, whether it concerns our home and family or our businesses and jobs.

Colossians 3:23 says, "Whatever you do, work heartily, as for the Lord and not for men,"

Philippians 4:13 says, I can do all things through Christ who strengthens and empowers me."

Jeremiah 29:11 says, For I know the plans and thoughts that I have for you; says the Lord, plans for peach and well-being and not for disaster, to give you a future and a hope."

Habakkuk 2:2 says, "And the Lord answered me, and said, Write the vision, and make it plain upon tablets, that he may run that readeth it."

Your Storage Room:

Malachi 3:10 says, "Bring the full tithe into the storehouse, that there may be food in my house. And thereby put me to the test, says the LORD of hosts, if I will not open the windows of heaven for you and pour down for you a blessing until there is no more need."

Deuteronomy 28:12 says, "The LORD will open to you his good treasury, the heavens, to give the rain to your land in its season and to bless all the work of your hands. And you shall lend to many nations, but you shall not borrow."

Your Guest bedroom Room:

The guest bedroom is often used for overnight guests. This is a place where people can rest and relax. Hosting people in our home has been a special blessing and a privilege. Over the years, we have hosted friends, family, and strangers alike. In the process, we have truly encountered angels.

In Matthew 25:35, Jesus says, "I was hungry, and you gave me something to eat, I was thirsty, and you gave me something cool to drink, I was a stranger and you invited me into your home."

Hebrews 13:2 says, "Do not forget to entertain strangers, for by doing so some people have entertained angels without knowing it."

Matthew 25:35-40 says, "For I was hungry, and you gave me food, I was thirsty, and you gave me drink, I was a stranger and you welcomed me, I was naked, and you clothed me, I was sick, and you visited me, I was in prison, and you came to me.' Then the righteous will answer him, saying, 'Lord, when did we see you hungry and feed you, or thirsty and give you drink? And when did we see you a stranger and welcome you, or naked and clothe you? And when did we see you sick or in prison and visit you?' And the King will answer them, 'Truly, I say to you, as you did it to one of the least of these my brothers, you did it to me."

Your Deck or Outdoor Area:

Jeremiah 29:5 says, "Build homes and plan to stay. Plant gardens and eat the food they produce."

Imagine drinking coffee early in the mornings on your deck, remembering that.

Lamentations 3:23 says, "His mercies are new every morning."

Or you are maybe having dinner outside while listening to some music?

Psalm 23:6 says, "Surely goodness and mercy shall follow me all the days of my life."

1. How can you set your home atmosphere?

_____

_____

_____

_____

_____

_____

_____

_____

_____

_____

_____

You have the ability to speak into existence on how you want to see things and how things should go in your house because that's where your peace resides.

2. What areas of your home do you think that you need to start with and why?

_____

_____

_____

_____

_____

_____

_____

_____

_____

_____

_____

_____

Conclusion

IN CONCLUSION, I AM so grateful that you took the time to invest in yourself and your home! My mother always told me to keep a clean house. I pray this book has blessed you and allows you to clean your house with the word of God!

I pray that this book has blessed you because your home atmosphere matters! God will not communicate an atmosphere of evil and self-righteousness.

My prayer is that your home is where you have peace on earth, that everyone who enters your home will feel the love of God, and that they will leave your home changed.

My desire is that you not only emerge from this prayer book changed and with a prayer strategy specific to your home on how to prayer-proof your home.

P-Praise

Gratitude to God for who he is and what he has already done should thread throughout every prayer because, ultimately, His name and fame are the only reasons any of these matters! Allow the Holy Spirit take residence in your praise at your home. Every piece of furniture should drip from the oil of God.

R-Repentance

Expect prayer to expose where you're still resisting Him, such as His commands and the manifold blessings and benefits He gives to those who keep His commandments. Let peace be the fragrance of your home.

A-Asking

Make a request now. Be personal and specific. Write down details of your own issues and difficulties as they relate to why your house is not in order.

Y-Yes

All of God's promises, the Bible says, have been fulfilled in Christ with a resounding YES!

Prayer allows God's words to be accentuated in God's own words from scripture. His promises to you always correspond to your needs. Nothing is more powerful than a woman of God using God's own words to prayer proof your home. — Dr. Rico A. Wagner

About The Author

*D*R. RICO WAGNER, AFFEC-
TIONATELY known as Lady, is
the wife of Sammie L. Wagner Jr.
who is the Pastor of New Foundation Church
International. She is also the mother of their 4
children, Samyah, Stephon, Tyler and Ian. Dr.
Rico is the Visionary of Desert Rose Women's
Ministry. Dr. Rico A. Wagner is devoted to New
Foundation Church International along side her
husband Pastor Sammie L. Wagner Jr. where she
assists her husband with various duties to en-
sure that his God-given mandate is carried out.
We believe in 2 Corinthians 5:7, "for we walk by
faith, and not by sight."

Index